Sudan's Angels

Hi Richard
Thank you for your
support of this book
Happy Reading ☺

Sudan's Angels

Maria Chisolm

Maria Chisolm

2/9/18

authorHOUSE®

AuthorHouse™
1663 Liberty Drive
Bloomington, IN 47403
www.authorhouse.com
Phone: 1-800-839-8640

Published by AuthorHouse 06/05/2012

ISBN: 978-1-4685-7453-1 (sc)
ISBN: 978-1-4685-7452-4 (hc)
ISBN: 978-1-4685-7451-7 (e)

Library of Congress Control Number: 2012905856

About the Author

Writing has been a part of Maria's life since she was ten years old. She started with journal writing. Back then it was called a diary. In the sixth grade she was introduced to haiku and later started writing poetry. Maria does occasional open-mic poetry readings around New York City, where vibes can be explosive and ecstatic, and where she has had the opportunity of making wonderful friends. She went to college at *Woodbury University* in Los Angeles and *The New York School of Interior Design.* She enjoys spending time with her boyfriend, cooking, reading a good novel, shopping for jewelry and interior decorating items, and traveling abroad.

About the Book

Sudan's Angels . . . is a compilation of many topics. It reflects how I see subjects and situations spiritually and organically. It is a book fiercely passionate about human beings, and our struggle as a people in this universe. I am a story-teller poet. So in this book you will read stories, monologues, poetry and essays. I enjoy the journey of writing poetry. I coddle it then give it its blessing for it to stand on its own. I have meticulously selected material that hopefully meets the Readers expectations.

Contents

Dedications

Sunrise Series

Love

Erotica

About Someone

In Thought

Essay

Soliloquy

Monologue

Fun

International Tragedies

Acknowledgements

Miss Elizabeth Carren was my sixth grade teacher who introduced me to Haiku. Norman Riley was my first acting coach and creative writing instructor. Evie Aviles always listens to my poems I read to her. David Carol took my Authors Photo. Whayne Clayton feels that everything I write is wonderful. Steve Martin for saying, "don't tell people what you do. Tell them what you are-a Poet." David Marshall introduced me to authors to read and who has given me eighteen years of his committed friendship. Dana Villarte who was my "Check in Coordinator" for my book and Leigh S. who did my "line editing" and Monica Reese was my "Design Consultant" Barbara Clarke who edited my first manuscript and Nella Chanoine who proof-read, giving final touches to my book. Andrew Joseph did the colored art design. Bubba Bill Jackson took my book cover photo.

Dedication

This book is for Barbara Clarke, Miss Elizabeth Carren, Norman Riley, and Steve Martin, who kept me in the light of writing.

Dedications

Dancing With Daddy
(for my father)

I hear the sounds of the tap dancer,
memories from my childhood.

He wore a black suit and bowtie,
a top hat and a twirling cane with
white rubber tips and a smile,
always a smile for the camera.

He had jokes to tell and songs to sing and
yes, there were showgirls with flashy headdresses,
pantyhose legs with low-cut and high-cut skimpy wear.

Joe Chisolm
Peg Leg Bates
Lon Chaney
The Clark Brothers
Sammy Davis Jr. and
Gregory Hines

I hear the sounds. *Tah-Tap. Tah-Tah-Tah-Tap.*

Ya know when I was a little girl,
I used to watch my father tap—so exciting!
He had people to speak with, appointments to keep,
busy, busy, busy in the limelight of show business
around the world!

One day he took my hand and we danced.
He taught me how.
I had black patent leather shoes, a mini skirt and
a white blouse with my hair always pulled back.

We had rehearsals
over and over again.
"Can you hear it?" He'd ask.
"Can you feel it?" He'd ask.

I would struggle, trip, and fall,
lose count.
I wanted to get it right—
and I did.

ah-Tap. Tah-Tap. Tah-Tah-Tah-Tah-Tap!
TeeTee-TeeTee-TeeTee-Dap!
Tic-e-dee Tic-e-dee Tic-e-dee Tic-e-dee Bah!
"And slide." *Dah-Dah!*
"Bring it back."
Click Click Bah!

"Posture." He reminded me. "Focus and count."
1 and 2 and 3 and
1 and 2 and 3 and
1 and 2 and 3.

Loosen up. Relax.
Move Move Move Dance!"

Ticky Ticky Ticky Ticky Tah!
Tah-Tah-Tah Ooow!
Ticky Ticky Ooow!
Bah Ooow. Bah Ooow!
Ticky Ticky Bah!
Tah-Tah!

"Don't curve your shoulders.
Where are your arms?
Hips! Let's see those hips!

I know you have blistered feet
but keep smiling. Always smile
for the camera because that's
show business little girl!"

Oh, what a life he had. Signing
autographs. The write-ups and the photographs.
It was the extravaganza of it all!

Yet in time, people slow down. Ailments creep and set in.
Being three thousand miles away from him and a call:
"It's cancer.
Please come."

"Don't stop breathing." I said to myself on the plane.
But he did. Just a few hours before we got there.
In the chapel room at rest, he was a
perfect picture of success.

I saw in him, vulnerability, family and friends.
I saw gentleness, freedom, and quiet.
And I remembered how we danced years ago.
We made it real back then.

ticky ticky tah, tah tah tah
ticky ticky tah tah tah tah
ticky ticky tah tah tah tah

> *Joe Chisolm*
> *Peg Leg Bates*
> *Lon Chaney*
> *The Clark Brothers*
> *Sammy Davis Jr. and*
> *Gregory Hines.*
> *Click Click Bah!*

Joe Chisolm, photo taken by Ron Howard approximately 1981

Song-And-Dance Man
(for my father)

"We only go to see a show so we can watch a song-and-dance man!"
Daddy sang those words for over forty years.
A tap-dancing man on the stage, he tipped his hat and twirled his cane,
told a few jokes and sang his refrain: the song-and-dance man.

He loved his work. It was what he did best.
Charmed every audience, which was never a test.
A wink of his eye and the ladies did suggest-
a song-and-dance man.

There were no drugs or booze or cigarettes.
Very clean. So refined.
Everything was groomed, polished, and shined.
I was proud to know that he was mine.

Oh, his extraordinary life:
Meeting the queen. Singing in Japanese.
Going to the Fiji Islands was Daddy's extreme.
African Cuisine for the song-and-dance man.

Mr. Entertainer and the Cabaret Shows!
Feathered hats on doll faces made him all aglow.
Pretty skirts and sassy smiles—how show business turned its dial,
and their hearts were always to a song-and-dance man.

Yet as the days and years went by, age crept in.
He took one deep breath, holding the hand of the angel of death.
There were no whispers. No shouts.
Sometimes promises. Sometimes there were doubts.

I saw him in my head; The charm he spread.
And if you listen, you will hear,
Tap-dancing feet in your ears.
Tap-dancing feet.
Tap-dancing feet.
Tap Tap, the song and dance man.

Always
(for my father)

He got dressed.
Shoes shined.
Hair trimmed.
Cologne splashed here and there.
Nails manicured, on his way to the highway,
the wrong way,
always.
Yes, the casino.
It was his home. His sanctuary.
His pride and joy, and on bad days
when he lost, it was his worst demon.
Sure, he won, but the thousands he lost
brought him fear and turmoil.
Having to face his wife who asked
over and over, "Please stop."
Thousands were gone but he always went back.
Daddy loved to gamble.
The excitement and passion;
The control and power.
The feel of the dice in his hand—roll it, roll it, bam!
For a gambler, tomorrow is always another day.
Another chance to win.
He didn't drink or curse, but he loved the women who passed,
pussyfooted or shimmied by,
who just went by,
always.
He wasn't a fine man, but neat he was.
Tailored and tucked.

He knew to do it right on the outside.
He knew when to go and how to spread that Chisolm flair.
The chips were stacked just right.
Cards were shuffled under the beaming lights.
That was the casino world and gambling was his disease.
Ain't no joke, daddy died a poor man, but we loved him.
We loved him
Always.

Caesar
(For Adolph Caesar)

The flowers,
their colors,
their sizes, their shapes
arranged so beautifully
for that man
in his grave
with grace.

They walked,
They walked,
twelve men in black suits,
carried a treasure, marched in their boots.

An actor,
a voice
so distinguishable
and renowned.
Charming to the utmost,
a captivating frown.

They walked,
They walked,
and carried the silver case.
People dressed in ties and lace.

A strong
and proud man,
dedicated to the
arts,
his style and technique
earned high ratings on the chart.

Yes they walked.
They walked.
Twelve men in black suits,
placed the case down, young man played the flute.

He's gone now,
where flesh went to ashes
and ashes to dust;
and I wondered
why the special ones
always had to be rushed.

They walked,
They walked,
Twelve men in black suits;
They were all in time, adding one more soul to the grey line.

They say it isn't how long
one lives,
but the quality of one's life;
and now in his passing
I know he will shine
in the light.

The Hours

(*For Lisa*)

And the pain wouldn't let me go;
And the pain wouldn't let me go.

I got married in a castle,
What a glorious day that was;
rose petals were scattered around,
continental breakfast and coco in mugs.

We honeymooned in the Virgin Islands,
sandy beaches and champagne.
Making love through the day;
yes, all the sugar was in his cane

We bought a house to live in—
Our house was a home of peace.
We worked hard and planned the future,
winter nights cuddled with our fleece.

We knew we wanted children.
Starting a family was a plan.
It was time to get started;
practice was slow, listening to old jams.

Found out I could not have children—
The music played a different tune.
Yet he and I, all we wanted
was to wash baby spoons.

Life will always be what it is.
Fate is not always controlled;
It is the hours that we go by—
the future always unfolds.

I tried the meds to help conceive,
but we believe they made me ill.
Not only did babies not come,
but cancer instead—no thrill.

And the pain wouldn't let me go;
And the pain wouldn't let me go.

I looked at the locks of hair in my hand,
so weary and fatigued;
Weight had fallen off me.
What other tragedy could succeed?

Not much time did I have,
we made the arrangements before I left:
Darling, cremate me and
let's meet on the sand in the next.

Many friends came to see me.
One sat down to rub my feet, and
I asked her for a pedicure.
So kind of her. So sweet.

The day before my calling
I moaned loud and long.
Tossed and turned and irritated—
I wanted to live and be strong.

And then there was no sound.
Quiet I finally was.
The angels came and lifted me;
I was flying with white doves.

Because the pain had let me go;
Because the pain had let me go.

Deceived

(*For Cousin Loretta*)

She was a wife in Brooklyn.
A mother of four,
in her grandmother's brownstone, on the top floor.

She was a young thirty-four,
twenty-five years ago.
A healthy, strong woman, always aglow.

Her husband, good-looking,
same age as his wife.
Construction was just a part of his life.

He always hung in the street.
Drank with buddies on the block:
He filled his days jiving with his flock.

She planned family barbecues,
block parties too;
Coordinated neighborhood birthdays,
cooked the winter stew.

She was life on top of life.
Steady in her game.
People tried to be like her, wanted some of her fame.

Separated from her husband.
Tired of the shit that had gone down.
He said, "Baby, please don't make our life a ghost town."

She had given him many chances.
She always took him back.
She didn't see a reason that time, to bend or slack.

We hoped she would keep her word,
never let him back in.
For that one night he asked, with that salacious grin.

She loved her husband, true, and
they shared many beautiful years.
But things grew so ugly, with so many tears.

They argued about little things.
Compatible no more.
Being with each other had become such a chore.

But still the question arose:
Would he charm himself back in?
Would he flavor all those adjectives to continue his sin?

Mr. Man was doing drugs.
His wife sang the blues.
She had hoped that he would stop. Didn't want that bad news.

He no longer made her toes curl.
No more taking care of the kids—
Not the man who was so suave; his roll was on new bids.

He knocked. She opened the door.
And how they won't forget,
the dinner table was so pretty, it was all set.

A couple of weeks had passed.
Not together with her man.
Something with her wasn't right and that's never in a plan.

Her balance wasn't steady.
She had shortness of breath,
ran a slight fever—just didn't feel at her best.

Back and forth to the hospital.
Doctors couldn't guess.
How she'd been full of life before this sudden distress.

Sent home many times for weeks.
Her strong body grew weak and frail;
Her husband tried to pamper but to no lasting avail.

Admitted to the hospital then,
back and forth from home.
We all sat so uneasy and listened to her moans.

The morphine helped somewhat to calm,
and mostly eased her pain.
Her sister couldn't stand to hear how she wheezed her name.

Her vision had gotten hazy.
Her skin flaky and dark.
Her fingernails turned yellow as her babies played in the park.

Her lungs had problems functioning
without an oxygen tank.
The tracheotomy so uncomfortable, she lay, her mind gone blank.

A serum from Africa arrived:
A last resort.
It was how she handled the battle, a soldier on the fort.

Whispers of what she may have had.
Morphine steadily upped; what had
happened to her sister? It all seemed so abrupt!

Her husband sat by her side.
Wondered how and what—
But then, he ran himself ragged; what about all his cuts?

She had lost a lot of weight.
Body was always hot.
Not much appetite anymore and she cried an awful lot.

She told her sister, "I'm scared.
Demons have come to tease."
Her sister told her clearly, "The Lord will put you at ease."

Then the call when the family was home:
"Patient not pulling through.
Come as quickly as you can, and expect no good news."

She passed on before they got there.
Husband at her side.
No one knew the answer; only guesses why.

About five years later,
sister saw the news.
A few documentaries that gave her some clues.

Loretta died of AIDS.
Seems her husband was slick;
He was the carrier while he messed with chicks.

He killed four women with it—
Eventually he knew he had.
He died ten years later . . . and yes, we were all glad.
The only regret her sister had
was that she died not knowing,
but why her sister would be glad,
is that her children and their children are healthy and growing.

Remembering
(for Steve Martin)

I stopped at the museum,
our meeting place.
You sat over there, remember?

We looked at all the exhibits when I arrived.
Talked about our day.
Laughed a little before my subway ride home.

Two years now. I hope you're resting well.
Still, in my mind, I see you at the window
and I will always remember.

Bonsai Tree

Sitting Under The Bonsai Tree

I am sitting under the bonsai tree,
chanting to my loved ones
who have settled in their eternal resting places.

The tree is fifteen feet tall
and the trunk grows in the same distorted manner
as the miniature ones.

I see them sipping chardonnay
planting ganja leaves
and never sweating.

They are laughing and joking
in circus tents
with rose petals that fall.

Heaven is what you make it;
Heaven is what I see,
sitting under the bonsai tree.

It sits on the horizon
perfectly in place,
like pink clouds floating to the east—

I will be there.

Crossing Avenues Of Colors
(*For Steve Martin*)

We met in the subway and developed a kinship
that thrived on honesty, simplicity, and laughter—
and we laughed while we sat on a rock,
free spirits,
and drank seltzer water.

Our thoughts focused on building towers in Central Park,
to employ all unemployed black folks
who could wear jeans and Gap shirts every day.
What would Donald Trump
have to say about that one?

We knew all about truth, a force
teaching kindness and laughter.
We met and talked and read and discussed the powers that be;
we created sounds, made masks of faces of angels, gods, and royalty;
we sat and meditated from the lessons of Kahlil Gibran.

We thought the way that prophets did or do.
Generated ideas on how to become holy,
because we were friends and friends made a difference.
Friends seek and find and cheer the winner and praise the loser so at the end of the day,
we laughed and sat on a rock, free spirits, and drank seltzer water.

There was no sickness or disease in our imagination;
We imagined health, wealth, crystals, and gold,
and the freedom to ride bareback on a deadly animal
in a land where people practiced Kama Sutra with a sting and
contortionists would be confused.

He wrote stories and photographed the colors and rhythms of Harlem;
He was a brother my senior,
with knowledge, desires, and a hunger that explored
the curves and scents of a woman.
And while he ventured and always found,

I moved to my own beat:
I canoed in the river while feathered fans cooled my brow.
I sang Hari Krishna to the waste that left my body in the cornfields at midnight.
I journeyed with gypsies to see exactly where they really did go.
I climbed Mt. Everest and cried out loud at the top of it to purify me.

My body and mind were strong.
My horizons broadened to higher planes;
I had to tell my friend.
To share with him the languages I learned, the food I tasted,
and the brighter stars that shone outside of my home land.

The one thing I didn't learn was how to cope without my best friend.
He had taken ill while I was away;
No one wrote me to say.
Brutal pain he had and there was no cure.
He was too far gone.

His cancer eased him into another dimension
of time and space and energy;
He said,
"Tell her I'm laughing,
sitting on a rock drinking seltzer water."

Tears I shed so hard.
So uncontrollably, that I shook, screamed,
I hit my shoulders,
my arms, my legs;
I paced the floor and hit the wall and saw blood.

I held myself and then held my breath,
and it came to me: "Hey, stop all of this.
We planted blueberry trees on the sidewalk of 108th Street;
We roller bladed down Fifth Avenue;
We touched the chambers of each others' hearts;
We enjoyed life, so all is well."

Steve and Maria at Countee Cullen Library approximately in 2001
for his photo exhibition.

The Writer And The Snapshot Man

(for Steve Martin)

Friends are a wonder.
Friends are bubble-gum sweet.
Fun times with ten dollars and nine, that's all I had that was mine.
But it didn't matter: Museum walks. Cafés in New York.
Folks dancing on the sidewalk.
The movies we bought.
Smiled while we talked.
Drank a drink and thought of poetry.
Cause that's what friends do.
He was my best friend.
Me being the writer and he the photographer:
It was about art and positive vibes
and the flea markets that filled our lives.
He took pictures of Harlem's rhythms and colors,
self portraits, and a few of me.
Chinese cuisine was our favorite feast,
dining as though we were king and queen.
Linen napkins and Mikasa plates, in the apartment on 108th.
Proper names of silverware? Just give him some plastic,
he didn't care. So was it fair that colon cancer killed?
It knocked. It deceived. It metastasized. It never did leave.
He called and said, "It hurts."
And I asked, "Where?" And he said,
"There." And I asked, "Did you take?"
And he said, "Yeah! But the pain is still there. I'm going into the hospital."
"Well," I said. "They'll take good care.
May I?" "No!" He said. "I need a day or so.
I need for this pain to just let me go!"
"Okay." I said. "Okay."

And it came to me . . .
If he goes away, if he goes away, if he goes away.
I ran outside. I needed to breathe. "Oh please God," I said.
"Don't take him away from me. There's so much to discuss.
The intimidation of the war. My book isn't published.
It still sits on the floor. Maybe my wedding day. Or maybe yours."
My legs were heavy. My soul grew dark,
wondering if the pain he talked about still stabbed him so sharp?
Sometimes we become weak and fall to our feet.
The chemo didn't help, there were months of it;
His torture left and then came back.
Nothing was relaxing on those restless nights,
but when friends asked, "What's up?"
He said, "Oh, I'm doing all right."
I had flashes of remembrances of how we met and where.
It's funny how we only think of those things
only in times of despair.
I will tell the doctors they lied!
Pull up his chart and make it clear:
The writer and the snapshot man are still here!
The hours were slim as death prepared for the cancer to kill.
No surprises. It will.
His body became cold as he tossed and turned,
and then the angels came peacefully and carried him
into the light. He was so peaceful. Had taken flight.
And I promised, there will still be
all those things we did, I and he.
I'm still gonna be me.
I'm still gonna write the truth and tell you what I see.
'Cause that's what
the writer and the Snapshot Man
will always understand.

Sunrise Series

Sunrise One

(*For Abdulbarr*)

It roared silently
Louder and Louder
Creeping up from the east
Birds chirped their tunes
Rocks formulated their color and the leaves began to rustle
The action was slow and a new day had begun
Her eyes opened because she heard the moment of the sunrise

Sunrise Two

In the heated tropics
a man in island jewels
wrapped in colorful cloth
stood facing east

Drum beats
thundered from the village
he listened and captured
the moment of the sunrise

Sunrise Three

She was in a sari with her arms stretched wide
feeling a cool breeze brush across her face
Within seconds a radiant shine beautified the universe
It was magnificent
It was her meditation
at the moment of the sunrise

Sunrise Four

There is a lake in the park on 110th and Fifth Avenue
The dawn is still
In front of the lake she stands
The picture of quiet marks the essence of her being
Beauty seen and felt is her attraction

A crystal light came from the east
slowly covering the water like
a blanket of magic
and the earth awakens to a new day
Her serenity at the moment of the sunrise

Sunrise Five

It was a cold morning on my way to work
riding the Liberty Line bus
I sat down and rested my head on the cushion
All was well
A passenger boarded and brushed against my arm
and I awoke abruptly while looking to the east
The orange sun shone so perfectly across the Hudson River
like a picture to be painted
I became warm
I was content
It was the moment of the sunrise

Sunrise Six: Soul-Mate

And here you are in the same room as I
I am so ultimately astounded

Please give me a moment to look at you and feel the curls of your hair with my fingertips
What glory personified

I look into the face of someone I'm in love with
shush it is the moment of the sunrise—

Love

Rhythm And Blues

(For Langston Hughes)

Love is a knife stabbing me in the heart,
not the smile that baby dolls have.
No, never the smile that baby dolls have.
Love is only pain that leaves me scarred.
Not raindrops dancing on roses;
No, never raindrops dancing on roses.
Love is tears heavy on my face,
not the jitterbug going all night long.
No, never the jitterbug going all night long.

Feel Good

I want to hear his voice always.
Like any flavored lollipop I crave;
I want to lick it, listen to its deep and sexy tones,
caressing on my funny bone.

I want to hear his voice always:
Telling me silly stories,
reciting Shakespeare and saying my name
for no reason.

I want to hear his voice always:
In the shower when I bathe,
in the street when I walk,
and when I dream of him.

I want to hear his voice always:
Whispering sweet everything in my ears,
how it soothes me.
How it strokes my back and kisses me without touch.

Just let me hear his voice always.

He Sang To Me

(for Tyheen Kynto)

In the supper club, the lights were low.
The champagne bottle was chilled
and the band was ready to play their tunes . . .
He sang to me.

I've got see you, somehow.
Not tomorrow, right now.

I watched his lips form each word, so soft and nice,
like a silk cocoon safe yet shivering.
Yes, he sang to me.
His voice was as smooth as satin and cool like a summer breeze.

My heart skipped a beat
when I caught the kiss he blew.
Three cheers
for the man who knew.

I know it's late.
But wooah, I can't wait.

He was radiant.
A little shy.
Tears came to my eyes
as I listened to his melody.
I swayed.

Yes, I swayed and
I wanted to touch me there,
because he sang to me.
Yes. Oh yes.
He sang to me.

So come on and steal away.
Please, steal away.

The Waiter Man

It was a winter's night when I was feeling . . .
Well, I didn't have too much to do.
I decided to hit my Friday spot on Tuesday after work.
There was always soft music that played,
and I sat at the end of the bar alone and had two drinks, slowly.
And that Tuesday evening with my drink in one hand
and a cigarette in the other while I sat on that high stool,
I saw him, the waiter man.
He had a glow from head to toe.
Come with me, I said to myself.
Take my hand. My order is love to go.
I wanted to drown in that man
who seemed so right that night.
The way he leaned over,
then walked over there, over here.
His demeanor. His gestures.
The way he wrote on his pad.
His posture. Those jeans that he wore.
Oh Mister Waiter Man, come and freak me if you can!
I put the spotlight on him when I peeked through the dark.
My right leg crossed over the left. And quickly
I became a mess.
Right then, I needed to rest.
The bartender asked if I wanted another drink
and I mouthed "No thanks," and put my cigarette out.
Fishnet stockings and black suede pumps,
I wanted to dance for him. Right then on that
counter top, I knew the show could begin.
Put the spotlight on me, I thought.
You won't forget a thing that you see.

Sliding. Grinding.
I would give the best that I could.
Newly ventures were aroused.
Odd creatures were stirred.
If I danced for him, would he even observe?
Ah . . . the waiter man.
I walked out and felt different,
more relaxed. I didn't go back.
My partner was waiting at home—and
fantasies can always create a different world.

Cuban Love

(*For Rudy*)

He held open the door of a silver Rolls Royce,
and I looked at him. He was wearing a white
linen suit and Eternity cologne
permeating the air, and so deliciously gorgeous;
He swaggered to the T with a grin
that illuminated and awakened the heavens, with
not one strand of hair out of place,
glistening like bubbles in champagne, and
full dark chocolate lips.
He wore a diamond pinky ring
on his right hand, with his left in his pocket.
I was divinely bedazzled by his presence;
I thanked the sun for radiating his blackness
with such exquisite perfection that it was a delight to have said,
"It's a pleasure to meet you";
And when he closed the car door after I sat down
I knew I would be driven to enchantment
never seen before.

On Wednesday

There he is, leaning against the building,
watching the rush of the tireless city . . . waiting.

My heart, pounding faster;
I am excited, knowing that he will touch me soon.

I sashay closer to his back and a scent of melon, rose, and orchid,
fills the air, it's china musk.

I gleam, shimmer.
He remembered to wear it!

He kisses my cheek and we walk,
exchanging glances and sentiments that soften the soul,

escaping into an evening
still sun-lit.

Erotica

Valentine Eve 2007

Long thrusts and strokes: you rode my back.
And danger was on two sides, yours and mine.

Remember how we did it slow, going with the flow?
We went on and on that night . . . and yes you did bite.

In the public restroom, ladies heard my sighs.
You caressed my body; I undid your tie.

I told you what to do? You, a perfect screw.
Then we woke up at a.m. and started all over again.

Now I don't see your face. No touch.
No embrace. You were over there and I'm here,
remembering the days when you were once near.

Your hands that roamed like an octopus.
Octopussy on your track.
Quietly I screamed. Quietly I attacked.

You stimulated me and activated my switch.
Your whore, this sexy, sexy bitch.
Kisses everywhere. Always wet down there.

You said you didn't want to stop. We had so much time,
tic toc. You mounted me on the wall. Front and back, I wanted more!

Our heads swayed. We rocked the beat. Didn't always finish between the sheets.
Bliss in the air. Do you remember how we did it easy-in the chair?

Remember how you had that right?
Exercised it, it was tight. Juicy Juicy on my knees.
Yes I always wanted to please.

There was no life outside our walls.
Our love inside insisted to pour.

Just remember how we were,
when you left and went to her.

Valentine Eve 2009

His rap always made me feel good—
Like lace lingerie good;
Chocolate kisses all day long good;
Masturbation in a bubble bath good;
Grab my hair and make me feel real good.

His rap was sly, soft, and nice.
I felt like a queen dipped in gold,
only wearing his bow tie and my garter belt.
I smelled his musk oil and was pleasured
lasciviously and I liked that.

His rap was easy, wet, correct.
Like I just had to have it,
how it slayed me so slowly—
His rap rang bells in my head.
I just had to bow down to him.

His rap was good!
Like good girl turned bad girl good;
Like tootsie roll suck all the time good;
Like eat me right there good;
Like frisky temptation good.

His rap had similes and metaphors and adjectives
playing on the pentatonic scale.
It was tight!
It was shaped to fit me just right. Like
debauchery in a castle, eating caviar between toes.

You see his rap was like
feathers on my neck, dreams
come true and manna from
heaven. It all just moved me
as I felt galvanized by the
feel, sound, and smell of his rap.

Black Shade Down

She was bombastically aroused by suitors
who came to see her one by one,
whom she inhaled as a nocturnal feast
with an enamoring gumption,
and later, how entranced she was viewing the video on playback.
When angels view those archives,
will they shame her lustful bliss
for men who had already wed others?
Or will they applaud her youthful frolicking
and draw the black shade down?

About Someone

Joey

"Jo-eeey!" a man yelled.
He was walking on Fifth Avenue.
"Jo-eeey!" he kept yelling.
His angry face was red and scary
and I wondered who Joey was.
A little brother in the army? A young man who once was?
Or maybe a sister who drowned—
He watched her take her last breath and saw her body submerge,
then sink to a slow and dreadful death.
Or perhaps he was Joey, wrestling with demons within.
Hearing stories in his head, wondering if then,
if he were living amongst the dead.

Footprints On 40th Street

(for the homeless man on 40th Street)

A man who is sitting on a midtown
Manhattan sidewalk has a stench so foul
that it can seep and settle into the nostrils of anyone who walks by.

He wears a pair of dungarees halfway down the crease of his black ass;
His naked belly is big and round while he rotates a glob of mush in his mouth,
not wanting to swallow it.

He appears to be in his late thirties,
medium height,
hair nappy and uncombed.

He sings no songs and recites no scriptures,
nor does he ask for favors from passersby,
nor does he play an instrument on all flat keys;

He is simply a man who sits or stands
and stares and looks as though he is trying to figure us out
while we are trying to figure him out.

I see him spread-eagled out on the ground
fast asleep with a dirty bundle of whatever next to him;
It probably is the only thing he has left in the world.

His feet are thick-crusted cheese, toes yellow and green in between.
Rotten sores that have eased up past his ankles,
grotesquely eating away at his flesh.

Somehow he has gotten lost and misguided;
Maybe he has fallen into a safe place in life where he walks quietly
and speaks to his shadow that follows him,

away from the corruption and deceit and vindictive games that people play.
He hears no comments and bows to no king or queen
who grace the line of his domain;

He is what he is:
A homeless man,
who makes footprints on 40th Street.

I Know What It Feels Like To Cry

I know what it feels like to cry.
Remembering how I lay in a fetal position on the bedroom floor;
I squirmed with heavy breath, and everything and everyone meant nothing anymore.

I know what it feels like to cry
because my heart pounded hard that night.
I felt the venom ease out of me as I screamed loud and long, *Why why why why?*

I know what it feels like to cry;
I wanted to punch the wall until I saw blood. I never wanted to hear that voice again.
I wanted to pack the pain in a box to send it to an island with no return.

I know what it feels like to cry.
I hit my leg until I saw it was bruised; I rolled from side to side,
embracing the scratchy fibers from the carpet and felt the pain ease out of me.

I know what it feels like to cry:
When I saw her sitting on a fire hydrant, bent over, tensely holding a cell phone.
Her face was red. Her small hands shook as she wept uncontrollably.

I saw her wipe the tears from her face.
She stomped her foot and dug it aggressively into the ground.
I wondered what was wrong.
Maybe a death in the family?
Maybe he left her while she stood alone waiting in the rain?
And I wondered . . . did her pain feel like a knife being twisted inside?

She cried with no sound.
She buried her face in her hands and rocked her head left then right.
I wanted to offer her a tissue;
I wanted to read her prose,
maybe place flowers at her feet, or touch her shoulder gently to console.

I saw how a voice trampled over her.
She didn't hide her despondent state.
She didn't shield herself with armor.
She didn't yell or ask for help from anyone.
She just sat, defeated.

I know what it feels like to cry . . . do you?

The Bar On Weber And Avenue H

(for Arnold)

Men gather,
wanting to enrich their lives
in a smoked-filled room.

They are men who can cry,
laugh and
some who get lost in their dreams;

They huddle for hours, listening to each other
brag about their adventures and heroism
in places they've never been.

Some listen to sea shells; some believe that love
really does last forever, as they lounge and
indulge in vodka with ice cubes silver,
yellow, and pink.

They guzzle and sing and drift away,
red-eyed and weakened by those spirits,
at the bar on Weber and Avenue H.

Then they go home to tell
their wives and girlfriends
more of their drunk, bad-breath lies.

The wine eats them, haunts them;
they drink more, then chase their own shadows until the walls cave into darkness—
The bar is a place where time is spent to forget and be subdued;

To get a pat on the back and tell a joke just to get them through,
walking on the same ground, sharing the same pain. There is a
feeling of belonging;

To hide and prophesize their spiritual beliefs with no regret.
To watch sports on the tube, cheering the winning
and calling those who are not "assholes."

The music is loud enough that not even high fives can be heard;
It draws them in, riding on vibrations that capitalize on their buzz,
that forever whisper, *Go ahead, have another at the bar on Weber and Avenue H.*

One more round for the boys in town,
and then the bar will close like always;
The gate will slide down and the locks are fastened at each end.

Some will have long walks home and some won't see home at all
but all will return tomorrow to the spot,
the bar on Weber and Avenue H.

In Thought

Hmmm

Sometimes when you meet someone slowly,
the time after meeting passes quickly.

When I Die

When I die, line my box with poetry and songs;
My spirit will feel free and will dance for you just a little.

Invisible

It rained outside and I had been pushed to the side
and the reasons didn't matter anymore,
I was invisible.
You see, I tried to talk to you.
Tried to express the what and the who;
But I kept it within myself,
put the cap back on, put it back on the shelf.
And the tears I shed, no one did see.
I kept expressions, the knots and trials, locked up inside of me.
You thought because I was happy all the time, that I didn't have issues.
Well, I had them just like you do.
The pretty house and the precious jewels,
and all those trips—
Didn't mean I had it all.
Just had a few gold chips.
I wanted to take it back off the shelf and open the cap.
Being so mournful, so tired of all the crap,
wanting to take that endless nap.
Friends were sometimes there. They were iffy anyway.
They messed around with your head, like lovers, they liked to play.
Family I didn't want to bother. I sat and prayed.
Smelled the odor in my grief: something bad had decayed;
Took the cap off those pills and said good-bye anyway.

Oh, and thank you for the beautiful bouquets. I saw you in the march.
You were all dressed so smart and I was the one laid down in grace.
Being in the world was such a lonely place.
It rained outside and I was pushed to the side,
and the reasons didn't matter anymore . . .
I was invisible.

A Thursday Visit

(*For Janet and Joe*)

The Thursday visit was spent doing tequila shots with lime,
musing from one topic to the other,
giggling about some things and nothing at all.

We ate cookies and buffalo wings and
she admired the red polish on my nails
and I told him that the music was sounding real good.

We three played bridge,
marveling over each one's agenda for the weekend,
listening to the rain crash down onto the skylight.

We realized then that life—
well, life should only be
a Thursday visit.

Essay

. . . And So I Write

Joseph Carey Merrick, whom we know as the Elephant Man,
had a congenital physical anomaly.
Sarrtjie Baartman, who died in 1815,
had elongated labia and large buttocks.
Both persons were exhibited as sideshow attractions or freak show performers.
They were laughed at, poked at for medical examination,
and touched inappropriately by audiences
misconstrued by malicious minds who didn't want to see or feel their perfect souls
. . . and so I write.

Elizabeth Glaser died from a blood transfusion.
Arthur Ashe died from a blood transfusion.
And Alvin Ailey died from a terminal blood dyscrasia or AIDS.
All three persons and millions of others—
whom by now, you knew, or knew of—
passed on from this disease, which affects nearly every organ in the body.
It is considered one of the most devastating
public health problems in recent history.
. . . and so I write.

Malik Brown, age fourteen in 1982, didn't survive a beating to the head;
Jesse Ramirez, in Phoenix, whose assailant had no motive,
was beaten and killed;
B. Jackson, also fourteen, did survive a beating—
Like the others, beaten by a baseball bat—
But Jackson slowly staggered home, bloodied, battered, and blinded for two months.
He was a victim of mistaken identity,
but the damage had already been done.
. . . and so I write.

Virginia Woolf, one of the modern literary figures of the twentieth century,
suffered deeply from depression,
several nervous breakdowns,
and suicide attempts.
She was plagued by mood swings.
She ended her life at fifty-nine by putting stones in her pockets
and walking into the River Ouse
while swallowing her persecutions for the very last time.

Ernest Hemingway was an American writer and journalist.
He was a giant of words who committed suicide by shooting himself with a shotgun.
He had homes and was well traveled;
He came from a history of successful achievers;
He was debonair, charming, and well-coiffed,
but something else too—depressed him and that
depression enabled such a genius
to splatter his brains out from his perfectly chiseled form.

Phyllis Hyman, an American soul singer and Tony-nominated actress,
was an exquisite beauty, voluptuous, and a class act.
She was gracious and fiercely passionate about her work.
But like many, she suffered with bipolar disorder and depression,
was an alcoholic and had weight problems and financial issues.
She lost her mother, grandmother, and a close friend within a span of one month.
And like the others above, felt lonely.
They felt sad. They felt defeated. It seems the more one has in life, the deeper the pain
. . . and so I write. I have to write. And do.

Soliloquy

I Have To Write

I have to write because I saw a little girl,
maybe eight years old, with braids unraveled in her hair
and clothes that hung loosely from her skinny shoulders,
smelling musty, crusted lips, and shoes that were too big
with holes on the sides, and scratch marks on her face,
who sat quietly next to her mommy on the F train going south.

I have to write when I see the homeless pushing shopping carts
with bags taped up, holding all they have left in the world.
They stand on corners, bathing with water saved in bottles,
trying maybe, to look decent for passersby, but
smelling like feces that sought sanctuary
in folds of their bodies that are known and unknown.

I have to write when I read Langston Hughes and Paul Dunbar
and Robert Frost and Elizabeth Barrett Browning
and when I hear novice poets like Robert Gibbons and Amber Atiya.
Their words gratify, praise and rejoice in my head.
Words that are organic that feed and fill me as I sit frozen in wonder,
and hear a symphony at its highest crescendo, applauding their humble magnificence.

I have to write when I see Alvin Ailey Dancers move and sway and leap and twist
and pose and glide into pirouettes and sit into plies
and stretch into an arabesque, then jazz it with "*Revelations*",
with "*Wade in the water. Wade in the water children.*
Wade in the water, God's gonna trouble the water."
Oh, they are perfect and smooth and graceful like kites that sail and birds that fly.

I have to write when I hear a father shook his baby: it
just won't stop crying, so he shakes the baby a little harder,
and the head flops back and forth like rubber and the father—
So enraged because he knows he can't pay the bills,
just had a fight with his spouse, not enough food on the table and
just not feeling connected with himself anymore—and doesn't realize the
breathing has stopped.

I have to write when I fall in love—it will be forever.
There will be shooting stars and Christmas cheer, mistletoe, all year!
There will be touching and holding and rose petals on bed sheets and kisses
even when there are bridges to cross and highways to drive over.
Our devotion will be warm and secrets will be none; the sky so blue,
a love nest for us two.

A head shot of Barbara Clarke, Maria's Mother, taken in London approximately in 1965.

. . . And That's Poetry

I hold the little boys close to me and tickle them.
Their giggles are contagious and delectable.
Four and seven years old are my nephews and when
I look into their faces, marshmallow treats are sweeter than cotton candy . . . and that's poetry.

On the dresser, sits a black and white photo of my mother. How she
oozes with softness and theatrics while perfectly posed against the
door ajar. Her shoulders purr with seduction, in her v-back dress,
with her cat eye makeup and delicate porcelain fingers, timeless . . .
and that's poetry.

I saw a homeless man across the street from where I was standing.
I watched him rummage through the garbage can on the corner;
He looked old and tired and so used to the street life.
Out of the trash, he took flowers then pushed his cart down the street . . . and that's poetry.

The end of a long day, the bath water was hot, the bubbles green,
the canton aperitif smooth, and so I drifted
to worlds away from this one, and then I saw you looking at me, I
looked at you back, and we smiled. Sometimes words are not needed.
. . . and that's poetry.

Quiet Expression

A woman once said,
"I don't like children;
They're dirty,
They ask too many questions,
they take up all of your time and spend all of your money,
and after giving them years of love and attention,
they express no appreciation."

One day a four-year-old girl and her family
moved next door to the woman,
and the girl asked,
"Miss, excuse me;
may I come with you
while you walk your black dog?"

The woman paused when she looked down
into a chubby face with curly hair.
"My mom says it's okay;
She's sitting right over there."
"Well then," the woman paused,
"Yes, you may."

The girl placed her hand
into the woman's;
The woman flinched when she
felt the gritty hand in hers
but she was okay and held on tighter
as they walked and
talked about little things.

Monologue

Bus Ride

(*For my mother*)

I rode past 82nd Street yesterday. I was on the number 11 bus on Columbus Avenue. We lived in a brownstone on the southeast side of the street, my brother and I and our mom. Her bedroom was the first-floor window. I wondered if the apartment was currently occupied. I was twelve years old, and we lived there for twelve years, a railroad apartment with seven rooms. It was a lot of fun then, and of course we had a lot of experiences. I remember when my brother discovered a dead rat as big as a possum in the cabinet underneath the kitchen sink. He was about fifteen years old then. You see, at first he didn't know if it was dead or just playing possum, and later he told people how he chased it, stomped it, and stabbed it two times before that big ole rat possum was dead. But he and I both knew that it was the mousetrap that killed it, and he went across the street to get somebody to take it out of the house. That thing scared him! Scared me too. He tried to get me to look at it under the sink, but no way; I couldn't do that. Shoot, the vision of that would have stayed with me for the rest of my entire life! He still remembers this as though it were yesterday. Mom of course, appreciated that it was gone when she got home.

Mom was real busy back then. She worked in retail for her bread and butter and also did what she loved most—she was an actress, a show-business gal. So there were actors always over for dinner parties or casual get-togethers: Roxie Roker, Ron O'Neal, Cleavon Little, Melba Moore, and Garrett Morris are a few names I can remember. Oh, they were stylish and elegant black folks. It was a period when black actors had a special unity about them. They ate together, partied together, rehearsed a role together. Mom was young and full of sophistication and expression—and really, she still is.

82nd street makes me feel nostalgic because I remember sitting on the stoop with friends during the summer, when TV wasn't enough. I remember going to the corner store for Mom—which is now a restaurant—for a Cadbury's Fruit and Nut bar, with the hope of getting four squares instead of two. I remember the man who lived across the street who would yell out of his fourth-floor window about being a prisoner and his hope that his ancestors would come to rescue him.

My stop came and I got off the bus, knowing that the memories of those twelve years would always be a part of me, and that it would always be safe to revisit those memories for as many times as I needed. Because it is the past that has made my future, and the future shines so brightly . . . like 82nd Street still does.

Fun

I Am . . .

I cry
I laugh
I giggle
I dance
I am Bohemian
I am the Queen of the Nile

I am
I am
I am

I am the bitch you'll wish you never met
I am the claw that will tear your skin
I am the liar who will do so to your face
I am the note that you will sing
I am the nudist that you saw that day

I fear
I seek
I find
I play
I am woman
I am tired of bullshit

I am
I am
I am

I am blind to what you do
I am a book you will want to read
I am a tree watch me branch out
I am a mountain please-climb-all-over-me
I am paper write down a story

I try
I sing
I explore
I am stronger
I am water color and sound

I am
I am
I am

I am soft, but rough when I want
I am blood that never wants to leave you
I am the hour that you wait for
I am the dream that you pray for
I am a test—and you have failed

I suggest
I move
I cheer
I pray
I run

I am
I am
I am

I am the coc that sweetens your caine
I am the grape that you sip in your wine
I am the friend that you will never be
I am the bye that will bid you adieu
I am the love that you have thought about

I listen
I watch
I touch
I see
I hear

I am better than
I am the shake
I am my own shimmy

I am one and so I am and
I am and
I am and
I am and

I in I and
I in I

Women Visit
(For Phyllis Chesler)

As we sat and shone in our glee, we spoke about many things,
how we've loved and lost, dining with kings—
Color them violet.

We were so chic in our draped attire, our jewels Tiffany's best.
In that evening of that hour, it was enchanting to be her guest—
Color us pink.

And our souls were rich with life, a magic tale we'll tell,
how our lives were always such, whistles and many bells—
Color us red.

As we sat, good food to eat, wine and Perrier too.
Crystal glasses to drink from, for dessert a delicious fondue—
Color it brown.

And as I sat I looked at her, the years had served her well.
All her worth and goodness, such a lovely *mademoiselle*—
Color her green.

And then she said to me out loud, "You're elegant and so charmed.
I think all your dreams became dandelions dancing on a pond"—
Color them orange.

And oh how her perfume permeated, the scent of violet and musk,
the trails of floral magnificence, sugar blown at dusk—
Color it purple.

Then the hour to say goodbye, the visit a pleasure indeed;
kisses and hugs, so long overdue, but finally achieved—
Color it blue.

I Write Poetry

I write poetry in the chambers of my chateau in Africa,
a beach view while I jest with the family croc, Sage.
I write poetry as a queen dripping in precious jewels,
wearing colorful chiffon and toe rings.
I belly-dance to my rewrites,
hearing drumbeats that sanctify me.
Trees whisper conceptions to questions I ask;
It's how I communicate in this poetic genre.
Diamond soil tracing down my thighs;
I mix the soil with a splash of the river,
creating a paste to feed this brown skin some of nature's wonder.
I write poetry because the angels have asked me to.
Poetry teaches me how to pray facing the mountains;
Poetry allows me to hear the moment of the sunrise.
I write poetry to do or do not.
I hear it; I feel it,
while blue sapphires are sewn into my corded braids and
red rubies are glued to my fingertips.
Poetry is how I seize the day,
how I watch the small children at play.
I write poetry to express—
I *am* poetry,
the rhythm and the beat,
the counting of the seconds,
gliding through the sky with my arms spread wide-
Poetry speaks to me.

I'm Going To The Barbecue

I'm going to the barbecue.
It's twenty-seven hours away.
There will be solitude, wine and cheese,
nude sunbathing—I can't wait for that day!

I'm going to the barbecue.
Blue Ocean all around,
I'll be at ease, cell phone off;
oh, I'll be getting down.

I'm going to the barbecue.
I know I'll want to stay.
Round tub, novel reading,
sky won't ever be grey.

I'm going to the barbecue.
A seaplane will get me there.
The Maldives Islands, temperature hot,
but I'm gonna be prepared.

I'm going to the barbecue.
Stilt Villas all in line.
Palm rooftops, stingray watching,
weaving skirts from vine.

I'm going to the barbecue.
I'll be lying by the pool.
hanging lanterns, food galore
Will be the rules.

I'm going to the barbecue.
Every year would be ideal:
Private hot tub, fresh air,
it will all be so surreal.

I'm going to the barbecue.
Swing slow on the hammock,
never wear a watch.
Bare feet on sand, no dirty socks.

I'm going to the barbecue.
Will pack my bag today!
Hurry now! Paradise awaits.
Ya know, I think I might stay.

I'm Taking The Long Way Home

I'm taking the long way home.
When I'm tired, I'll grab something to eat;
Stop at a bookstore, jewelry store, a florist;
Bowling if I feel like it, or horseback riding as a treat.

Maybe skateboarding through Central Park,
a picnic, the theater, ride the carousel.
Feed the pigeons if I feel like it, or
shop at the mall.

I might walk across the Hudson,
waving to the yachts.
Think of what play to write,
imagine pink bows on my socks.

I'll admire the architecture,
Romanesque, Rococo, the designs inspiring to see.
I'll take pictures if I feel like it,
build my own Cathedral like he.

Side-saddle on an elephant.
Pucci Sunglasses and a stogie to smoke.
Fanning feathers will cool my brow;
no fire there to stoke.

A body massage with aromatic oils,
a manicure, eyebrows, a facial and tea.
That's right baby;
I'm only thinking about me.

I'm taking the long way home.
Maybe stop off at that mans house
for love. Some jazz will soothe our
souls, replays on how it all began
and enjoy every moment of that road.

Sketch by Andrew Joseph

Women

Sassy, funky, big-hipped jazzy women.
Pot-belly pretty women.
Long-haired, short-haired, messy—or nappy-haired women;
Curled or permed haired women.
Bashful, trifling, stuck-up bitch-witch women.
Smart, brainy women;
Rich, powerful, presidential super-women.
Struggling poor women.
Pocket-book-clenching, dress-swaying, naughty women.
Proud gay women.
Aristocratic, problematic, systematic, melodramatic women.
Heterosexual easy women.
Cry-baby, no-backbone, shallow, petty women.
Smelly crotch-scratching women.
Secret women.
Flower women.
Music women.
Water women.
Canvas women,
who fight and love aggressively, passionately, like the rambunctious bad-asses that they are!
One seed.
One planet.
One love . . . women.

International Tragedies

Tsunami

People at play,
People at work;
People walked,
People loved,
People vacationed;
Children in school—
People were happy.
Families were at home
And then the sea and the storm and the waves
Came strong and washed people away.

People in fear,
People scared;
People floated on trees,
They held onto each other.
People were once at many
*And then p*eople were counted:
One
Two
Three
Four.

No hope,
No warning,
No time,
No direction to run.
And so people cried;
People were hungry;
People were tired;
People were missing and people were dead
because the sea and the storm and the waves
came strong and washed people away. Yes,
the sea and the storm and the waves came
strong and washed people away.

Emmitt Louis Till, "in a photograph taken by his mother on Christmas Day 1954, about 8 months before his murder." (Photo from wikipedia)

Emmett Till

(for Emmett Till)

Boy, why'd you whistle at that white girl?
I say boy, why'd you hafta whistle at that white girl?
They'll getcha for that, in Money, Mississippi.

Men pounded on his front door.
Took him from his bed at night.
Said he had to be properly identified in Money, Mississippi.

Young boy never did go back home.
The men beat him in a weathered shed.
Shot him. Barb-wired his neck to a cotton gin, in Money, Mississippi.

His mother had his body sent home. Thousands viewed the disfigured corpse.
"You will see his face!" She cried.
"Look what they did to my son!" in Money, Mississippi.

Fourteen years old, that's all he was.
Clouds still puff in the sky, and the Tallahatchie still flows
like a matter never was, in Money, Mississippi. In Money,
Mississippi.

Children Walk

Every morning
little food to eat;
Not feeling up to going on that beat.

Wake in the morning,
No shoes to wear,
not always cheerful faces, siblings look and stare.

Flies always follow them,
they seem to take the ride.
Sticking on their shoulders,
sticking in their eyes.

Does a young girl's innocence
get her snatched away?
Making her easy prey?

Children walk. No happy feet.
They walk for water till they are weak.
Six miles there, do they ever crawl?
Wonder how they make that trip at all?

Do they want to play?
Smell the grass grow?
Talk to the animals as they go?

Hauling water for their families,
never going to school,
hoping that God can help figure out new rules.

Not enough pads, so
menstruation is a problem.
Blood dripping down little legs,
a situation so bothersome.

Trying to hide it from Daddy,
do they puke from the heat,
wiping it from his feet?

Their lives are different from ours.
Their struggle is what we see.
I'm sure they count the hours to one day be like we.

Unclean water is worldwide.
Twenty kilograms carried on their heads,
lugged back home for grain and bread.

The diarrhea is what kills.
They drop and pass away.
Gentle children, pretty faces, perfect like a bouquet.

Do they know the King?
The Malcolm and truth?
Do they know they walked being so young in their youth?

Do they know Mandela?
Rosa Parks and Holiday?
Do they know that we love them and for them we pray?

Do they cry together,
cry themselves to sleep,
knowing that tomorrow again will be a repeat?

Children walk. No happy feet.
They walk for water till they are weak.
Six miles there, do they ever crawl?
Wonder how they make that trip at all?

Four Women in white veils from Sudan

Sudan's Angels

I see four women standing in the hot sun,
draped in white veils,
ashy bare feet, long toes, and I wonder,
how protected are they from the heat with no shoes or sunglasses?

I see them, teenage beauties:
Chapped droopy lips,
unprocessed hair—
It looks like brown cotton.

I see their faces.
Jet black eyes filled with promises not kept,
their expressions are lonely and still-
And I wonder . . .

Do they have enough food
to eat before they close their eyes?
Do they ever pray to the angels? Pray to the angels.
Do they ever pray to angels?

I see faces, doubt, fear, while gazing at visitors
with digital cameras.
Mechanical monsters:
Click-click. Click-click. Click.

I see these women.
Do they ever wish to carry Gucci while sashaying under ruffled parasols?
They don't have diamonds or pearls or powdered cheeks
or piercings in stretched earlobes.
No painted fingernails with tips.

And I wonder.
Do they run to the hills praying
in hope of one day to dance in Paris?
If terror destroyed their villages,
would stitching their mouths silence their screams?

Are they ever forced by men
who can viciously stroke themselves in and out of their sacred holes,
then smile when smearing their semen waste
on their bleeding hearts that hurt?

Sudan's angels don't wait for keepers to suit their schedule.
They don't wear Victoria's Secret, they don't pick private schools, don't carry Verizon,
and they don't ride in SUVs or stack designer shoes by color.
They are what we will never be and we are only what they dream about.

So you see, I see these women.
Beauty personified. Black skin. Red tone.
Markings distinguishing their tribe.
Eyebrows neatly combed on scowled faces in temperate heat.

Four traditional women in a gentle somber way move me.
So I continue to wonder.

Heal

Little girl from Africa
only three years old.
Hide and seek, big fun, her heart was made of gold.
She didn't know they would come.

Little girl from Africa just a baby girl.
She wore pretty dainty frocks, chose not to have any curls.

Little girl from Africa
she always ran and played,
laughed with her family, ate beans and grain in the shade.
She didn't know they would come.

Little girl from Africa was seized by three men.
Each took their turn, pushed hard inside her gem.

Soldiers used themselves and weapons;
she screamed even after they were done.
Little girl from Africa
didn't know they would come.

They asked her mother, "How does your daughter feel?"
The mother replied with tears, "She is learning how to heal."